THE EAST INDIA COMPANY

A History From Beginning to End

Copyright © 2016 by Hourly History.

All rights reserved.

Table of Contents

The English in the Atlantic Era and the Founding of the East India Company

The 17th Century: Struggling, Building, and Growing with Violence

The East India Company Enters the 18th Century

The British Government Steps In

China and the Opium Trade

Growing British Involvement in the 19th Century

The End of the East India Company

Conclusion

Author's Note

A brief word about terminology: The life of the East India Company spanned several centuries and went through internal and external changes. Thus, its nomenclature also evolved. While it began as Governor and Company of Merchants of London trading with the East Indies, its name then became the English East India Company. Its official name would change again with a merger in the early eighteenth century to United Company of Merchants of England Trading to the East Indies, though this name was never widely used. In addition, with the establishment of the Kingdom of Great Britain in the early eighteenth century (of which England was a part), referring to people and businesses as "British" became increasingly common and the company evolved to be called the British East India Company. To make the issue more complicated, several other European nations also had East India companies, including the French and the Dutch. Throughout this book, best efforts have been used to refer to the English company by the name that would have been most commonly used at the time (thus, when you read about the company in the late seventeenth century, it's referred to as the English East India Company, while at the end of the eighteenth century it will be referred to as the British East India Company), but at times alternate names have also been used.

Chapter One

The English in the Atlantic Era and the Founding of the East India Company

Most people raised in the United States are familiar with the North American story of British conquest and colonization. The failed colony at Roanoke, struggles at Jamestown, the pursuit of religious freedom at Plymouth Rock, taxation without representation, Boston Tea Party, American Revolution, and independence. But this is only a very small part of a history that begins much earlier, ends far later, and encompasses nearly every corner of the globe and dozens of other nations and peoples. In short, many Americans' knowledge of the British colonial era is fractured. Though you may not have heard of the British East India Company, it is a major part of that story.

When Christopher Columbus landed on islands in the Caribbean (believing he had reached the Pacific Ocean), it initiated what is generally referred to as the "colonial era" or the "Atlantic era." Initially, the conquest of the New World was dominated by Portugal and Spain; although Columbus was Italian by birth, he was funded by and represented the Spanish monarchy. Both wealthy Catholic countries ruled by monarchs, they not only had the funds to sail, fight, and settle, but also the military might to confront foreign competitors. While England was certainly powerful in the late 1400s and 1500s, it did not rival Spain and Portugal's strength. What is more, England was embroiled in its own conflict of conquest in Ireland throughout most of the sixteenth century.

This all changed in 1588 when the English Navy defeated the Spanish Armada. Philip II, the monarch of Spain and a devout Catholic, planned to overthrow Queen Elizabeth I, whose father, King Henry VIII, had broken away from the Catholic Church to form his Church of England. The Spanish Armada was widely and rightfully considered the most formidable fleet in the world, so when England proved victorious, it was a major blow to Spain's morale and a boon to English confidence. While Spain held onto its Atlantic empire, this victory emboldened the English to not only venture further into colonization in the Atlantic but also other potentially lucrative sites around the world, including the East Indies.

Thus it was in the euphoric aftermath of the victory over the Spanish Armada that Queen Elizabeth I accepted a proposal from London merchants to send ships to the Indian Ocean, where Spain was not as dominant. This first expedition was successful, in that the ships reached their destinations and returned home. A subsequent voyage in 1596 was not, but despite this failure, Elizabeth approved a third voyage in 1600 and granted the merchants a charter for their newly formed organization: the Governor and Company of Merchants of London trading with the East Indies (the Caribbean and surrounding land masses were still referred to as the West

Indies, even though Columbus' claim to have discovered a western passage to the Pacific was long disregarded).

The company was founded by 101 Englishmen who made investments in the new company, and each was entitled to an equal share of its value, making it an early joint-stock company. This newly chartered organization would be governed by a governor, Court of Proprietors, Court of Directors, and committees. The governor would be at the helm along with the twenty-four-member Court of Directors. The Court of Directors were appointed by the Court of Proprietors, and there were also ten committees that served underneath the directors.

This royal charter gave the founders and the newly formed organization, which would become the East India Company, a monopoly on trade in the East Indies for fifteen years. The East Indies were then bounded by the Cape of Good Hope on the southern tip of Africa and the Straits of Magellan on the southern tip of South America, meaning that all land east of the Cape of Good Hope and west of the Straits of Magellan were fair game, while everything else was off limits.

Royal charters were not uncommon during the colonial period, as they were mutually beneficial to both the Crown and those to whom they were granted. Those holding the charter enjoyed the benefit of a trade monopoly which was protected by the Crown, while the monarch essentially outsourced the risks involved with exploring, settling, or exploiting a new territory, which included at-sea disasters like shipwrecks and piracy, and on-land obstacles such as disease and unfriendly natives.

Therefore, the founders of the East India Company were willing to stake the finances necessary to open exploration and trade with the East Indies for England, and they would be entitled to whatever riches—minus taxes—they found.

Queen Elizabeth granted the new company a monopoly, but Elizabeth was only the monarch of England; in other words, only English law protected the charter, and only English citizens were compelled to obey it. The Governor and Company of Merchants of London trading with the East Indies faced stiff competition from other Europeans, especially the Dutch and their Dutch East India Company (VOC). Even though the Dutch East India Company was not officially incorporated until 1602, two years after their English counterpart, the Dutch had been a formidable presence in the East Indies for many years, as had the Portuguese. During the sixteenth century, the Dutch struggled against the Portuguese, who had dominated the spice trade in the region and against whom the English would also struggle. The Dutch who, like the English, were not controlled by the Catholic Church, worked with local Muslims to loosen the Portuguese grip on the trade. In the end, this waning of Portuguese power would also benefit the English.

Spices were the chief reason that trade in the East Indies was so valuable. The spice trade was very old, dating back into antiquity at least as far as the ancient Egyptians. It was a lucrative business that grew throughout the Middle East and Far East including cinnamon, pepper, and ginger. Other goods were traded along the spice routes as well, including opium and silk. It is also enormously historically significant for the cultural exchanges that took place along its paths: peoples from very diverse regions of the globe met each other along these trade routes. They expanded technologies, spread their religions, and shared their cultural knowledge. They became aware of how other people lived, spoke, and learned. It is impossible to overstate how important these exchanges were in advancing human civilization.

Prior to the sixteenth century, this trade took place primarily over land, which meant that Middle Eastern powers controlled European access to it. But with both technological improvements in shipbuilding and sailing, as well as navigational techniques, Europe was finally able to enter the trade as a serious competitor. They could completely bypass the Middle East and Mediterranean by traveling by sea.

So, by the time the newly chartered English company entered the trade, it was already well established, and Europeans had been active by sea for at least 100 years. Thus, the English East India Company struggled initially against entrenched competition. Sir James Lancaster commanded the company's first expedition after the charter in 1601. Lancaster was a skilled navigator, and just as important, he was also a shrewd negotiator, which helped him establish the first English factory in the region on this first voyage. While the East India Company called their outposts factories, they were not manufacturing centers, as we understand the meaning of the word today. For the East India Company, a factory was a center of trade and often housed company representatives and offices, almost like a headquarters or satellite office.

This first factory was built at Bantam after Lancaster forged an alliance with the Aceh peoples in present-day Indonesia. He made a follow-up voyage two years later in 1603 and remained a director of the East India Company until his death. After the 1603 voyage, he was knighted by King James I. As an interesting side-note, Lancaster also discovered that lemon juice could be used to treat scurvy during his first East India Company voyage on board his ship, the Red Dragon, though the practice of giving lemon juice to sailors would not be formally adopted for another 200 years.

During the company's first few years, Queen Elizabeth I passed away and King James I took the throne. Because the company was profitable, the new king initially broke their monopoly shortly after they had built a factory in India at the Bay of Bengal. He hoped that more companies competing would yield more profit. However, his plan did not work out, and in 1609 he reversed this decision and granted the company a charter and a monopoly that would be in place unless the company failed to turn a profit for a consecutive three-year period. Thus, the East India Company had not only survived its initial decade but now had the indefinite protection of the Crown, as long as the prosperity that saw them through their first ten years continued.

Chapter Two

The 17th Century: Struggling, Building, and Growing with Violence

The company continued its expansion in India throughout the seventeenth century. Several trading posts and factories were built as more and more company officials maintained permanent posts across the subcontinent. Eventually, forts and factories were established at Bombay, Madras, and Calcutta. The company achieved a major victory in 1717 when Mughal Emperor Farrukhsiyar granted the company a firman, which meant that the company no longer had to pay customs duties in Bengal. This firman gave the English a huge advantage in trade in India, and it also saved them a great deal of money that they were then able to re-invest in expansion.

But it was not always smooth sailing for the company in India; the 1600s saw conflict and struggle as the East India Company worked on gaining footholds and advantages around the Indian and Pacific Oceans. Let us explore some of the events of the seventeenth century that preceded the accomplishment of the firman.

Even though the company was protected indefinitely by James I's decree, it still faced formidable foes among other European nations, especially the Dutch and Portuguese. Over the ensuing years, the English would fight both nations in the East Indies for control over the spice trade. The company's first major victory was the naval Battle of Swally in 1612, in which they defeated the Portuguese. Although it was a relatively small battle that has seldom made its way into history textbooks, it is significant for several reasons. First and foremost, it broke Portuguese domination in India. The Dutch had weakened Portuguese strongholds throughout the Indian Ocean, but the English had been mostly unsuccessful in India because of Portuguese control. In addition, the victory also prompted the company to change how it financed itself, and it became a modern joint-stock company. Prior to this battle, the East India Company had primarily sent individual voyages, mostly to islands such as Indonesia. These had been individually funded, meaning that investments were made specifically for these individual voyages.

But after the English realized that they could make inroads into India, the company began funding itself with stock sales that were not tied to one particular voyage. This may not seem like a big deal, but it allowed the company to take on more dangerous ventures by essentially spreading out the financial risk; if one voyage failed, particular investors would not have lost their entire investment, which made investing in the company more appealing. Finally, the Battle of Swally was important because a few years after the 1612 victory, the Mughal Empire in India was enticed to open trade with the East

India Company, which they likely would not have been able to do if the Portuguese had not lost. The East India Company had now made significant inroads in the region that would give them a lucrative share of the trade in spices, silks, cotton, and other goods.

Another violent encounter occurred in 1623, this time with the Dutch, with whom the English and the East India Company would have a complicated relationship in the East Indies. After making inroads in India and parts of Southeast Asia, the English looked to expand their dominion. During this pursuit on one of the Spice Islands, ten Englishmen were executed along with ten Japanese men and one Portuguese man in what would become known as the Amboina Massacre.

The Dutch governor had believed that the group was conspiring to overthrow the Dutch on the island. After being tortured, they confessed and were executed. While this was a relatively small event that the Dutch considered entirely legal, it placed great strain on their relations with the English, ending any chance the two nations had at cooperation anywhere in the Indian Ocean, at least temporarily. Thus, the English East India Company was relegated—for the time—to the trade it had already established elsewhere, especially India.

It is important to pause here and note another violent aspect of the early history of the East India Company—that of slavery. British participation in the slave trade in the East Indies began by the 1620s, and primarily dealt in slaves kidnapped or sold from East Africa. Thousands of lives would be stolen to work in India and on islands in the region until the end of the trade, which would not occur for at least 150 years.

Additionally, British and East India Company representatives also enslaved native Indians. Even after Britain abolished slavery in all of its territories in 1833, an abusive system of contract labor and indentured servitude developed in India especially, which some historians have argued was akin to actual slavery in practice. This practice bound Indian, African, and other indigenous laborers to brutal work contracts that were sometimes impossible to escape. The growth of the English in India has certainly had an enormous impact on world history, but it is important to remember that it came at great human cost.

Due to the fact that they were shut out of trade with islands and nations that the Dutch controlled, the East India Company focused more intently on its growing interests in India. In the wake of the victory over the Portuguese in the Battle of Swally in 1612, the Mughal Emperor Jahangir granted permission to Sir Thomas Roe and King James I to build a factory in Surat, on the western coast of the Indian subcontinent. Surat is a strategic location not only because it is coastal, but also because it is on the Tapi River, which winds into central India and connects to other waterways throughout the subcontinent.

It is important to remember that at this time, India was not a unified country. While various parts of India were related and sometimes worked together, they also had individual rulers and governments with separate laws and decisions, and they sometimes warred with each other. Naturally, this created both challenges and advantages for the British, who could sometimes play one side against the other, but whose actions in favor of one kingdom might endanger their interests in another.

The problems that the East India Company faced did not always unfold abroad; they also endured domestic turbulence during the seventeenth century. The English Civil War occurred mid-century when King Charles I was overthrown and beheaded, and Oliver Cromwell temporarily headed a republican government. Cromwell protected the East India Company, recognizing its financial importance. When the monarchy was restored and King Charles II placed back on the throne, he granted the company even more privileges and power, including the right to coin money, wage war, and govern their territories largely independently. By the end of the seventeenth century, the East India Company was more powerful and independent than ever.

The East India Company also faced challenges from common Englishmen and women. In 1667, the East India House in London, the domestic company headquarters, was attacked by rioting weavers, who were enraged that Asian textiles were threatening their livelihood by driving down the price of domestic cloth and reducing their wages. This is a challenge that governments have faced again and again: whether to engage in free market trade and protect business interests or whether to enforce a tax on foreign goods, called a tariff, to help protect domestic manufacturing. In this instance, the East India Company initially backed off on their own volition, selling their products more aggressively elsewhere, but eventually, the English demand for cheaper textiles won over, and their trade resumed at the expense of English textile workers.

The East India Company always looked toward future expansion in India, which included seeking the firman that would provide such an advantage. Much effort was expended to achieve it during the late seventeenth century, and they sent their first governor of Bengal, Sir William Hedges, to parlay with Bengal's Mughal governor in 1682. However, because the company's general governor in London interfered in these negotiations, they broke down, and by the end of the decade, the East India Company was at war with the Mughal emperor. Their base in Bombay was attacked in 1690, and in order to avoid complete annihilation, the East India Company had to beg the emperor for forgiveness. Despite this setback, normal relations were restored and the company expanded into Calcutta.

While the East India Company worked on expanding and seeking a firman in India during the seventeenth century, they also made inroads into other Indian Ocean and Far East locations. Foreign relations were as complicated in the colonial era as they are now, and at times enemies worked together against common foes. During the Dutch-Portuguese War, the English and Dutch allied to oust the Portuguese from China. The Dutch had also assisted the English in their momentous defeat of the Spanish Armada in 1588. Even though the Dutch would remain fierce competitors for the East India

Company, this joint victory helped both the English and Dutch to expand into China.

The East India Company established a trading post in Taiwan in 1672, and the Chinese government, which sought to strictly control foreign incursion and trade, allowed the English to voyage to a few other locations, including Canton, where they moved their Chinese base later in the century. Like the royal charter that granted the East India Company an English monopoly in India, they were also granted a monopoly to trade with China that did not expire until 1833.

Another example of how foreign relations impacted the English East India Company was their relationship with Japan. In 1613, the company sent its first envoy to Japan. Captain John Saris met with Tokugawa Ieyasu and was able to establish a factory in Hirado. Just a few years later, though, Japan restricted the British to that location, barring future expansion. One of the causes was continued English conflict with the Dutch; the Japanese viewed Dutch-English fighting in their waters and ports as threatening. Thus, after the 1623 Amboina Massacre, the English factory was closed.

This decision on the part of Japan makes sense when you consider how suspicious the Japanese were of European encroachment on their domain. Japan has been remembered in the historical record as notoriously isolationist. Beginning in 1633, they initiated a policy of sakoku, which prohibited foreigners from entering Japan and largely forbade Japanese from leaving. While they were not completely isolated, as they did trade with a few other countries, including China and Korea, this policy protected them from the kind of colonialism experienced by China and India. Neither the East India Company nor Britain itself would resume trade with Japan for more than 200 years, until after U.S. Commodore Matthew Perry arrived in 1853.

Another setback for the English East India Company in the seventeenth century involved not another nation, but fellow English pirates. Today, our culture has romanticized pirates in films, television, and popular culture. But in reality, history's pirates were violent and out to make a profit. While their ships were somewhat egalitarian, crews were often made up of outcasts from various societies, or lower class workers with few other opportunities, rather than humorous career criminals. What is more, they often operated in ambiguous or fluid degrees of legality: what the British called a pirate, the Spanish might call a privateer in their employ and vice versa.

In 1695, as the East India Company neared its 100th birthday, Henry Every, a notorious British pirate who was nicknamed "The King of Pirates" in his lifetime, launched an attack on the Indian Mughal's fleet. In it, Every joined forces with five other pirate captains and their crews in order to raid the Indian Mughal Emperor Aurangzeb's fleet on its return from Mecca. This fleet was legendary at the time, certainly the richest in Asia and quite possibly the world, especially the ship *Ganj-i-Sawai*. It was also well protected and heavily gunned, so its capture by Every and his pirate compatriots was all the more stunning. A fierce fight ensued between the pirates and their victims when the two fleets met, and rumors of torture on the part of the pirates abounded in the aftermath.

The Indian emperor and the Indian people were enraged. In response, Aurangzeb attacked and shuttered four East India Company factories and imprisoned the officers of each, even though the company had no relationship with Every other than birthplace. In order to appease Aurangzeb and his government, and save the East India Company's Indian commerce, British Parliament refused to grant Every any kind of amnesty, and the East India Company offered a huge reward for his capture. He and his crew fled, and while a number of those involved in the raid were caught, tried, and hung, Every disappeared after 1696 and remained a wanted man for the rest of his life. His fate and place of burial are still unknown. The manhunt in search of him, as well as the rewards offered for his capture, helped smooth relations between this part of India and the East India Company.

Despite some setbacks and struggles, the first century of the English East India Company's history closed with tremendous growth; the company had several well-established factories and outposts throughout the Indian Ocean, was protected both by royal charters as well as an Indian firman and a similar Chinese edict, and looked forward to accumulating fabulous wealth. However, these achievements had not come without cost. The company optimistically moved into the eighteenth century and would play a key role in British expansion through the Age of Revolutions.

Chapter Three

The East India Company Enters the 18th Century

The British East India Company had survived its first century. It had also survived a very turbulent period in British history: the English Revolution and reinstatement of the monarchy, as well as institutional changes to Parliament. However, a new set of challenges awaited in the eighteenth century, which saw the empires of Europe grow at astounding rates. By the end of the century, nearly the entire globe had been touched by the spark of revolution, which spread across the Atlantic World and outward, touching nearly every major European power and thus impacting their holdings overseas, including their holdings in the Indian Ocean, the domain of the British East India Company.

The eighteenth century began with new challenges for the East India Company, and the British government would play an increasingly more active role in its activities. Shortly before the Mughal piracy incident, the East India Company lost its English monopoly in the region. While Britons had always been aware that India, China, and the islands of the Indian Ocean and Pacific were potentially lucrative trading partners, the wealth accumulated by the East India Company throughout the seventeenth century spurred many aspiring tradesmen to action.

By aggressively lobbying Parliament, they—along with some of the former members of the East India Company—were able to push the passage of a law that allowed any British company to trade with India unless Parliament specifically prevented them from doing so by identifying them by name. The passage of this law was remarkable given that the company and its officers had become very wealthy, and thus very influential in government, and had fought its passage.

Shortly after the passage of this law, another large company that would compete directly with the East India Company was formed. Even similar in name, the English Company Trading to the East Indies was partially funded by the English government. But the directors and officers of the East India Company were true capitalists, and therefore anxious to hold onto their control of trade in India. Because of this, they made a large investment in the English Company Trading to the East Indies, which allowed them to obtain a measure of control over the governing body of that new company.

While the two competed fiercely in some places and for some amount of time, the new company never posed a serious threat, and eventually, the East India Company would neutralize it, absorbing the English Company Trading to the East Indies in 1708. After the merger, the official name of the new company was the United Company of Merchants of England Trading to the East

Indies, though it would still mostly go by the recognizable name, East India Company.

As the company grew wealthier, they also grew more powerful. In order to protect their interests in the East Indies, they gradually established what would be akin to a standing army. Additionally, rather than working in tandem with Parliament and the English government, as they did through much of the seventeenth century, conflict grew, as evidenced by the above incidents involving competition. The English government wished to maintain some control of the company, especially as they behaved more and more like an independent body and grew larger. Meanwhile, the company sought greater autonomy, and especially after the incident with the English Company Trading to the East Indies, they realized that their best chances for achieving a monopoly might lie outside government.

The company also grew weary of the impact of British foreign relations, especially the strained relations with the French. North Americans refer to the conflict of the 1750s-1760s as the French and Indian War, but in reality, it was a global conflict most commonly known as the Seven Years' War, and it was in many ways a world war. It was primarily a conflict between the English and French, as well as their respective allies: in North America, these were various tribes of Native Americans, but both nations also had allies in other global locales, including India and the East Indies.

In fact, France had its own French East India Company (Compagnie française pour le commerce des

Indes orientales), which was founded in 1664 specifically to give the English a run for their money. The French company was near bankruptcy for most of its existence, but it nonetheless did compete with the English in some places, especially India.

By the time the Seven Years' War broke out, one of the East India Company's most consequential leaders was at the helm. Robert Clive would not only secure India for the East India Company, but was one of the most important early figures in British domination of the subcontinent as well. When hostilities between the French and English began, India became another site of conflict. The combatants and their Indian allies met fairly early in the war that broke out in 1754; the Battle of Plassey occurred in 1757.

Plassey was then the capital of Bengal, and it was headed by a still-independent Nawab who allied his territory with the French. Despite this battle being a huge victory for the British East India Company, whose forces fought in lieu of the actual British military, the 1763 Treaty of Paris that ended the war gave most of the French territory captured in the East Indies back to the French. In India, they were allowed to keep some military presence. However, the French military threat was virtually eliminated by the end of the eighteenth century, and this event greatly weakened it, despite rearing its head again during the American Revolution (the French entered the war on the side of America, against the British). So, while the Battle of Plassey did not have a great impact on the outcome of the Seven Years' War itself, it was extremely consequential for the British East India Company; it was the first step toward solidifying their control over Bengal by weakening the French and defeating the Nawab.

While the Battle of Plassey helped solidify English control of India over other European powers, it did not make relations with the Indians any easier. In that battle, the English fought the Nawab of Bengal, Siraj Ud-Daulah, as well as some other local leaders. These leaders were allied with the Mughals, who had granted the English East India Company their firman and had been important trading partners. However, warring with their longtime ally estranged the English and the Mughals. In the years after the Seven Years' War, the East India Company would increase its military force, especially in India, and relations would be handled in a more aggressive manner.

The Seven Years' War was a boon to the East India Company in another way: it distracted Parliament from involving itself in company affairs. Throughout much of the eighteenth century up until that point, Parliament had wrestled with the company. In addition to revoking their charter and helping fund a rival company, Parliament grappled with how to regulate the company's actions as they obtained control over more land and built a larger military force.

By the end of the Seven Years' War, the East India Company had a large standing army of about 20,000, something that both benefited and threatened the British. While the British military did not have to sustain the risk or the expenditure of protecting its interests in India, it did have to contend with the actions of a military force that sometimes acted in its name but was out of its control. What is more, the company employed mostly Indian-born soldiers, called sepoys, who, though they were trained by the British, did not necessarily have British loyalties on the battlefield. The British worried that, though the company acted largely independently, they still represented Britain, and could cause foreign relations problems. At the same time, though, Parliament and Britain were growing more dependent on the company; fifteen percent of British imports were from India, and almost all Indian imports came into the country through the East India Company. In addition, Parliament borrowed money from the wealthy company in 1742. And, as the Industrial Revolution in Britain dawned, British manufacturing came to depend more and more heavily on raw materials, such as cloth for the textile industry, produced in places like India.

In addition to the issues that the Seven Years' War caused for the company in India, the eighteenth century also saw the first of three wars fought by the British East India Company against the Maratha kingdom. These three Anglo-Maratha Wars would eventually benefit both the British East India Company and the British nation, serving to weaken Indian leadership on the subcontinent further. So, while they were fought by the company, they nonetheless benefited Great Britain in their eventual colonization of India.

The First Anglo-Maratha War took place from 1775 to 1782 and was, technically, an Indian victory, although it involved the company and the British government more deeply in Indian affairs. As is obvious from the dates, the British were distracted by the American Revolution in North America, as well as growing tensions with European adversaries, so they were comfortable allowing the company to act independently.

The war erupted over an Indian dispute over the succession of the Peshwa (the second-highest-ranking government official, a hereditary position) in the Kingdom of Maratha. The British East India Company pledged troops in support of the brother of the deceased Peshwa, Raghunathrao, in the Treaty of Surat, even though the deceased Peshwa had an infant son. Diplomacy broke down, and several battles were fought in the ensuing years. Finally, after long negotiations, the Treaty of Salbai was signed.

While technically a British loss, as they were forced to relinquish Raghunathrao, they kept Salsette and Broach, two new regions gained in the war, and perhaps more importantly, the Marathas agreed to block French trade entirely. In the end, these concessions probably benefited the British East India Company more than what they had given up. The peace would be short-lived, however; the Second Anglo-Maratha War broke out in 1802 and lasted until 1805, and the third took place from 1817 to 1818.

While each war obviously had its intricate issues, battles, and personalities, the general outcome is familiar. While Indians of many kingdoms and dynasties put up valiant fights against British encroachment, the company made further and further inroads into completely controlling the subcontinent.

The Marathas were not the only Indian kingdom that challenged the British East India Company. The Kingdom of Mysore in southern India also posed a threat, and the company fought four Anglo-Mysore Wars at the end of the eighteenth century, between 1767 and 1799. The conflicts involved other Indian kingdoms, whose loyalties sometimes wavered between the East India Company and the Mysore dynasty. The British East India Company was ultimately victorious, especially after their successful siege at Seringapatam and the death of the Tipu Sultan, one of the Mysore rulers. In the end, the Mysore Kingdom was broken up, and the company consolidated control in southern India.

This victory, along with ultimate victories against the Marathas and the Sikhs, would virtually hand complete control of India over to the British by the middle of the nineteenth century. In addition, the British East India Company involved itself in smaller disputes and skirmishes, often manipulating existing animosities between rival kingdoms and rulers throughout the subcontinent. They did this in order to further entrench themselves in Indian affairs, win concessions from more and more local governments, and eventually wrest control away from Indian leaders.

With the responsibility of ruling vast land holdings and millions of diverse people came challenges. Any colonial government faces these challenges, and even though the British East India Company was a company and not a state, they were not immune. One event, which drew outrage throughout India and in the mother country, was the Great Bengal Famine, which took place between 1769 and 1773. The actual death toll is unknown, but somewhere around ten million Indians died of starvation and malnutrition, one-third of the population of Bengal. What is more, and what drew the ire of some British reformers, was that the famine was largely caused by the East India Company's policies in India.

First, an oppressive and increasing land tax meant that many Bengalis had to sell foodstuffs or plant saleable "cash crops" to pay the tax instead of food that they would have subsisted on. To make this issue worse, the company reaped the rewards of this tax. Today, we hope that when we pay our taxes, the money goes to public programs that will benefit us in some way, whether it be road construction or education. But most of the tax money paid by Bengalis went into English pockets, out of the country, further impoverishing the region.

Because they were suffering so much financially, many farmers had given over their land to growing opium poppy, which yielded more money. The company encouraged them to do so because they were engaged in a very lucrative opium trade in China. But when the profits could not buy food, they were useless. As people starved and died, they obviously stopped working and producing, and this ate into the company's profits, though no amount of money can measure up to the human cost of this tragic event.

While the death toll outweighs any financial loss, the company suffered so much that they neared bankruptcy and had to turn to the British government for help. In response, Parliament passed the Tea Act in 1773, which is notorious in American history as one of the events that led to the American Revolution. While this act is usually taught as a tax on tea in the colonies, that is not quite accurate. The act actually allowed the East India Company greater leverage in its trade dealings with the American colonies. It allowed the East India Company to avoid paying taxes on tea imports, which drove their prices down compared with that of all other tea; most of the tea consumed by American colonists was Dutch tea, imported illegally.

Even though this made tea in the colonies cheaper, the colonists saw it as unfair to local tea dealers, and in a grander scope, they worried about this encroachment on their sovereignty. If the British Parliament could place this unfair exemption on East India Company tea purely for their financial benefit, then who knew what else they could enforce. The event led to the Boston Tea Party where East India Company tea was thrown into Boston Harbor, a major cause of the American Revolution. All of these events were truly global in scope, and the East India Company was very frequently involved.

Chapter Four

The British Government Steps In

While Parliament passed the Tea Act in 1773 in order to help protect the East India Company, they also saw the need for regulation. In their eyes, the company had grown too large and powerful and acted too much like an independent state. What was more, the company was one of the largest and most lucrative in the country, which made it not only important to the national economy (as further evidenced by the fact that Parliament was willing to step in to protect it), but also meant that many prominent Britons were investors or large shareholders who had a serious interest in the solvency of the East India Company.

The company had not paid its annual fee of 400,000 pounds to the government since 1768, which it was supposed to do in order to maintain its monopoly. Thus, the East India Company Act, or Regulating Act, was also passed in 1773. Some regard this as the beginning of the end for the East India Company, as it drastically reduced their autonomy and power; the government would now oversee all company affairs. The company's representatives and lobbyists in Parliament fought its passage but to no avail. The company was forced to essentially cede their territory to Great Britain.

The actual mechanisms of the act are complex, but simply put, it had seven main points that took aim at how the company was governed (it established a governor-general and a council, appointed mostly by Parliament, as well as a judiciary), and it prevented the company and company military officials from receiving gifts of any kind from Indians (which were essentially bribes, or illegally extracted). William Hastings, who would be removed from his post by an impeachment trial, was appointed the first governor-general. Despite the act's sweeping reforms, in the end, the corruption within the company continued. The act would be violated and instructions by government ignored until Great Britain took further action almost a decade later.

Eleven years later, Parliament passed the Pitt's India Company Act, also known as the East India Company Act of 1784, in response to the rampant corruption that continued within the British East India Company in India, despite the Regulating Act. In fact, the famous Irish author, politician, and philosopher Edmund Burke, who was also important to seeing William Hastings impeached, attempted passage of a more stringent law the year before, but the company's lobby successfully blocked it. Burke, a humanitarian who supported the American Revolution, was appalled at human rights violations committed against the Indian people.

Pitt's India Act attempted to divorce the company's trade activities from governance. In other words, the British government would take a more active role in the actual governing of India, while the East India Company would focus more on trade and commerce. In order to accomplish this, the act set up the Right Honourable Board of Commissioners for the Affairs of India, also called the Board of Control and the India Board, which consisted of six members, several of whom would be high-ranking British government officials. It was more successful than the council set up by the Regulating Act of 1773, and it remained in place until the British government officially took over the governance of India in 1858. However, overall it was a failure. The act was not clear, and lines between what constituted governance and what constituted commerce were often ambiguous, leading to confusion and conflict.

All of this involvement in company affairs happened as Britain faced many challenges itself. Aside from the East Indies and especially India, which were certainly eventful, Great Britain faced a series of serious events throughout the eighteenth century, mostly in their Atlantic Empire, that to some degree distracted them from events in the East Indies. The most well-known are perhaps the Seven Years' War and the American Revolution, but Britain was at war with other European nations almost constantly throughout the century, as well as dealing with domestic challenges brought by the Industrial Revolution.

In addition, at the beginning of the nineteenth century, Britain outlawed the African slave trade and by 1833 would emancipate all slaves in their empire. While from a human rights standpoint this was a monumentally wonderful move, it did lead to a decline in the British

Atlantic empire. As these issues settled down, Britain involved itself more in India and the East India Company. Thus, as the nineteenth century dawned and progressed, the British East India Company saw itself working more and more with—and against—an increasing British presence.

The next act of Parliament that dealt with the East India Company was passed only two years after Pitt's Act. Just a half-decade from his surrender in the American Revolutionary War, Lord Cornwallis was made the second governor-general. He was chosen because Parliament regarded him as loyal, honest, and incorruptible: in their eyes, just what the company needed. In addition to Cornwallis' appointment, the East India Company Act of 1786 also gave the office of governor-general more power, and more clearly demarcated the roles of government and company, so that the confusion of the Pitt's India Act would clear. Parliament would not interfere in company affairs again until the nineteenth century, except to renew their charter in 1793. However, the growing presence of the British government in company affairs was, in some ways, the beginning of the end for the East India Company. A little over half a century later, in 1858, they would lose all control of India and be effectively dissolved.

Chapter Five

China and the Opium Trade

The British East India Company expanded its presence in China during the eighteenth century, having already established a factory in Canton. Like in Japan, foreign encroachment made the Chinese nervous. Thus, they restricted foreign traders to the province of Canton and appointed only one group of traders, the Hongs, to trade with any and all foreigners. The Chinese did not make this arrangement easy on the Hongs; socially, they were ostracized, and their trade dealings incurred heavy fees and taxes. In order to protect their economic interests, the Hong merchants passed these costs along to the British, who had a trade monopoly with China which remained in place until 1833. Despite these levies on the trade, it was still extremely lucrative.

Many times, England is associated with tea in popular culture and collective imagination, and this would never have come to be had it not been for their exclusive trade with China. While Britain exported some goods to China, especially cotton from India and finished textiles, the British demand for tea was so high that it actually caused a trade deficit which, regardless of how lucrative the trade was, cut into the company's (and thus England's) profits. For that reason, the British government interfered in company trade—rather than administration, which had composed most of its encroachments in India—but their actions were on behalf of the company. King George III sent Britain's first ambassador to China to attempt to negotiate a more favorable trade agreement. Lord George Macartney arrived in Peking in 1793. Despite charming Emperor Qianlong and presenting many elaborate gifts, all requests made to benefit English trade were refused. A second mission in 1816 was equally unsuccessful.

Opium was a major issue in British-Chinese relations and in dealings with the East India Company. Opium is a drug that is typically smoked and acts like a narcotic on the body, and it was illegal in China. However, as previously discussed, the East India Company had run into financial problems because it was buying so much tea from China and had little to trade in return. So, they began illegally selling opium farmed from poppies in India, mostly Bengal, which also contributed to the Great Bengal Famine in the eighteenth century. Getting the opium into China was not simply a matter of hiding a little bit in ships or with other products; the amount of opium smuggled was massive and required intricate networks of smugglers, secret or disguised bases, subsidiary companies, and illicit communications. In essence, the East India Company became the world's first "drug lord."

While Britain would carry opium into China into the twentieth century, China did not go down without a fight. The First Opium War broke out in 1840 when China imposed the death penalty for smuggling opium. The war lasted almost three years and was a British victory; China was forced to hand over Hong Kong to Britain and open five new ports to foreign trade, and begin easing its restriction on opium. In the Second Opium War, from 1856 to 1860 (overlapping the Indian Rebellion that would effectively end the East India Company's reign in India), China was forced to legalize opium. While Britain would face competition in the opium trade henceforth, it would continue to provide a revenue stream. Britain's involvement in the opium trade in China would long be a source of Chinese resentment toward Great Britain for its detrimental impact on their society.

Chapter Six

Growing British Involvement in the 19th Century

Throughout the eighteenth century, the British East India Company consolidated control in India and increased trade in some of its other lucrative centers, especially China. As they did so, the company grew exponentially. So much so, that by the dawn of the new century, most of the work done was in administrative or management roles. While trade was obviously still vital, the company had gained control of so much land and so many people that governing and maintaining control was becoming more important in the day-to-day operations of the enterprise. In 1806, the company opened a college to train administrators, called the East India Company College.

As the century settled, and especially after the conclusion of the Napoleonic Wars, Great Britain turned its attention more and more to involvement in Indian affairs. The British East India Company had enjoyed a great deal of autonomy throughout the eighteenth century, despite the passage of several laws meant to reign them in. But this would completely end in the nineteenth century. Also, as the company grew and governed more and more territory and people, some of their practices were called into question. Notably, Indians chafed under discriminatory practices and attitudes. Mid-century, a rebellion broke out in India that effectively ended the company's presence there, handing control over to Great Britain itself. Let us explore some of the other events of the early century, prior to that momentous uprising.

As the territory that they controlled grew throughout the eighteenth century and into the nineteenth, the military strength of the British East India Company also expanded. The company maintained three separate armies, and by the time of the Indian Rebellion in 1857, this force numbered over 250,000. It had its own military academy, officially named the East India Company Military Seminary, but commonly called the Addiscombe Military Seminary in present-day London. The seminary opened in 1809 and was taken over by the British military in 1861.

Like the higher-ranking administrators, the company's military was also dominated by the British. While the lower ranks were filled with Indians and other native peoples, officers and higher-ranking soldiers were almost always of English origin. Naturally, this caused resentment among Indians and other peoples, and this cultural, religious, and racial disrespect and discrimination would be a major cause of the 1857 rebellion.

Being an East India Company officer was not an easy job, and the threats they faced were not always military. Throughout most of the eighteenth century and into the first few decades of the nineteenth century, India experienced a devastating cholera epidemic. The Indian death toll was innumerable; about 10,000 or 90% of East India Company officers died.

Most the consequential events of the nineteenth century for the East India Company involved Parliament and a growing government presence. While the Anglo-Maratha Wars and other conflicts fought by the company in the eighteenth and nineteenth centuries had strengthened their hold on India (by 1813 they controlled almost all of the subcontinent), they were costly, and the company was in dire financial straits again. Parliament passed the Charter Act of 1813 or the East India Company Act of 1813 which, while granting a 20-year charter, also reasserted British dominion over the company and all of its holdings. It also forced a growing cultural presence in India. The company had to finance education for India and allow missionaries in as well. In 1835, the English Education Act further compelled the company to provide education to Indian children.

In the grand scope of the life of the East India Company, 20 years was not a long time. However, the years between 1813 and 1833, when the charter expired, were monumentally consequential. The Napoleonic Wars officially ended, and the English Industrial Revolution took off. The British government was taking a more active role in economic activities, and the East India Company would not be exempt. While their charter was renewed for another 20 years, they lost their monopoly, and Britain was allowed a greater part in administration.

In the next two decades, the Government of India Act of 1853 was passed, which dealt another blow at the company. Instead of renewing their charter for a defined period of time, Parliament declared that India would be run by the company until they decided otherwise. This meant that the company could be taken over at any time. It is not hard to imagine the impact this decision had on investors, and recent historians have argued that this event was the death knell for the company, rather than the rebellion that officially ended its presence in India four years later. Regardless of which was more consequential, by mid-century, the end looked near for the East India Company.

Chapter Seven

The End of the East India Company

As conditions in India worsened for the Indian people, the East India Company came under greater criticism and scrutiny. As discussed, the British government involved itself more and more in company affairs in the eighteenth and nineteenth centuries, but the British public also worried about the poor treatment of Indians and even atrocities committed on the part of the East India Company.

Largely in response to the bad living conditions endured by the Indian people, a large rebellion broke out in 1857, which would spell the end for the East India Company. It is referred to as the Sepoy Rebellion or mutiny, the First War of Indian Independence, and the Great Rebellion. As one of its names implies, this uprising involved Indian soldiers of the East India Company, the sepoys, and a somewhat separate (though simultaneous) civilian rebellion. These sepoys were organized into three armies, and the company very much manipulated them by playing upon existing caste and religious tensions between Hindus and Muslims. Various issues caused unhappiness among the sepoys toward the company, especially Hindus of higher castes. While discrimination—especially when it came to promotions and ranks—and religious differences (rumors occasionally circulated that the British would try to force Christian conversion on their soldiers) certainly contributed to these tensions, the company also restructured compensation and expectations of service. Sepoys had been exempt from serving outside of India, but some changes to the duties of lower caste soldiers made higher caste sepoys fearful that they, too, would have to serve overseas eventually. The rebellion primarily originated with higher-ranking sepoys, so these fears and rumors had a great impact.

 The final straw within the military would come with religious and cultural differences. While not getting too distracted by the intricacies of nineteenth-century weaponry, the guns used by company soldiers required cartridges that had to be bitten to be opened. Rumors abounded that these cartridges were greased with beef and pork fat; eating beef is forbidden in the Hindu religion, and eating pork is not allowed among Muslims. At worst, the rumors stoked fears that the British intended to force conversion to Christianity on the army, but even at best, they convinced Indians that the British held contempt for their religions and way of life. Even though the British East India Company attempted to quell these fears by replacing the cartridges, soldiers believed this proved that they were right in the first place, and they did not trust that the new cartridges were free of the animal fat. The distrust created by this incident probably resulted from long-standing strained relations and mistreatment between the company and the Indian people; the fact that the Indian soldiers could not be convinced to trust the company again supports this possibility.

Religious and cultural differences also contributed to the rebellion among civilians. The East India Company, in its administrative capacity, attempted to force reforms on the Indian populace. Some of these included the role of women. They attempted to abolish the practice of sati, in which widows committed suicide to join their husbands, and allowing widows (those who did not commit suicide) to remarry. In addition, higher-caste and upper-class Indians also experienced anguish as their power and influence were ceded more and more to the British. All of this was also on top of a general sense of distrust of the British, who had mistreated Indian people and Indian land for centuries. Certainly, this kind of abuse had built resentment over a much longer period of time.

While the rebellion itself only lasted about a year, it was extremely brutal, and spread throughout the entire subcontinent. Atrocities were committed on both sides: rape, torture, dismemberment, destruction of civilian lives and property, to name just a few of the offenses that abounded. These atrocities on the side of the rebels were widely reported in Britain, especially rape, and dissolved any sympathy that the British people might have felt toward the Indians and their plight. The papers largely ignored any atrocities committed by their own soldiers, so the British public did not advocate for any mercy toward the rebellion. In fact, Karl Marx himself spoke out against some of the propagandized reports and questioned their validity.

As the company's British forces fought the rebellion, they had a blank check from the British people to use whatever means necessary to suppress the rebels, and since they were not technically British soldiers, they were not subject to rules that may have reigned in actual soldiers in the British military.

Regardless of the lack of sympathy toward India among the British public, Parliament recognized that the rebellion signaled that the British East India Company's practices were unsustainable in India, and in the long term, hurting British interests. Therefore, in response, Parliament began disassembling the company with the passage of the Government of India Act of 1858, proposed by Prime Minister Lord Palmerston serving during Queen Victoria's reign. The law effectively liquidated the company and handed over governance of India to the Crown. While many company employees remained employed, and the company's basic administrative structure remained in place, India was now officially under the control and protection of the Crown; the East India Company was no longer involved. It continued to engage in the trade of tea with China for several more years, but it was completely ended with the passage of the East India Stock Dividend Redemption Act of 1873.

Conclusion

Although the British East India Company was effectively ended in 1857 after the Indian Rebellion, its legacy was felt for a very long time afterward. While the company no longer had a presence in India, Britain certainly did. After 1857, the British government took over the roles that had been filled by the company, and India was officially colonized. The British military took over the East India Company's military force, and many company employees became employees of the Crown instead.

Without the East India Company and the inroads they'd made in India, it is doubtful that Great Britain would have gained control over the subcontinent as they did; Great Britain would be a colonial power of India well into the twentieth century, until after World War II. What is more, the East India Company established trade and agricultural practices that had long-lasting and sometimes devastating effects in India. Even today, India lives with its British legacy, for better or for worse. Because none of it would have been possible without the conquests made by the East India Company in the sixteenth, seventeenth, eighteenth, and nineteenth centuries, the impact of the East India Company is almost incalculable.

Printed in Great Britain
by Amazon